JOHN IRELAND

THE
COLLECTED PIANO WORKS

Volume 4

Stainer & Bell Limited acknowledge the ready co-operation of copyright holders in allowing works to be used in this collected edition and thank the John Ireland Trust for a generous contribution towards the cost of publication.

Foreword © 1976 Stainer & Bell Ltd.
ISBN 0-85249-396-7

STAINER & BELL

THE COLLECTED PIANO WORKS OF JOHN IRELAND

FOREWORD

Ever since the closing years of the eighteenth century, when Clementi, Dussek and J. B. Cramer settled here, London has been a major European centre for the composition and performance of piano music. John Field, Irish composer of the first piano nocturnes, was a pupil of Clementi; Field's contemporary, G. F. Pinto, wrote seven piano sonatas before his tragically early death at the age of nineteen. Their successor, Sterndale Bennett, the most important of the early English Romantics, gained international recognition while still a student at the Royal Academy, then in Tenterden Street. (Schumann, who was deeply impressed by Bennett's concertos and shorter piano pieces, described him as "a pianist above all things".) And it was in London that John Ireland, the greatest writer of piano music among our later Romantic composers, spent virtually the whole of his working life.

Ireland (1879-1962) studied composition at the Royal College under "that great man" Stanford. At the age of 17 he was appointed assistant organist at Holy Trinity, Sloane Street; in 1904 he moved to Chelsea, where he lived for nearly fifty years. Besides playing the organ at St Luke's Parish Church (from 1904 to 1926), John Ireland taught composition at the R.C.M. Among his pupils were many of the outstanding writers of the next generation, most notably Benjamin Britten.

Ireland had a great feeling for places and people, so it is not surprising that London and Londoners figure frequently in his music. He also loved the Channel Islands (*The Island Spell; Sarnia*) and Sussex (*Equinox; Amberley Wild Brooks*); in fact he spent his last years in a converted windmill facing Chanctonbury Ring on the Sussex Downs. Another major influence was the writings of Arthur Machen (*The Scarlet Ceremonies; Legend* for piano and orchestra). He also had a close affinity with A. E. Housman and Thomas Hardy, and his settings of their poetry are among the masterpieces of English song.

On one occasion Ireland repudiated the suggestion that he was a great composer, but added that he was "a significant one". This is a characteristic understatement. Ireland's piano music is as vital a contribution to the British tradition as is that of Fauré to the French; and the work of both composers (wholly personal, yet at the same time completely characteristic of their own countries) is an enrichment of the heritage of European music.

He had decided views about the performance of his own work. One interpreter, who studied over the years with the composer, has written: "Ireland's own playing had an intensity and finish that he expected in others. He was most particular about melodic lines, and would often mark copies with the pencilled words *firm, emphatic*, or *significant*. Tempo was always an important consideration; any sense of hurry was to be avoided. Whether the harmonic scheme was rich or astringent, chord changes had to be clearly heard, and rhythms had to be incisive."

The items in this collected edition are arranged in chronological order, with the exception of the Piano Sonata which is published by itself as Volume Five. Such errors in previous editions as have come to light have been corrected, with the assistance of Eric Parkin and Alan Rowlands. The complete solo piano works have been recorded by Alan Rowlands on Lyrita RCS 15, 23, 24, 28 and 29 (mono); the principal works by Eric Parkin on Lyrita SRCS 87, 88 and 89 (stereo).

GEOFFREY BUSH
Music Adviser, The John Ireland Trust

January, 1976.

ACKNOWLEDGMENTS

The following works are printed and engraved plates used by kind permission of the following:

The Cherry Tree, Cypress and *The Palm and May* from *Greenways.* B. Feldman & Co. Ltd trading as H. Freeman & Co.
Le Catioroc, In a May Morning and *Song of the Springtides* from *Sarnia.* Boosey & Hawkes Ltd, 295 Regent Street, London W1A 1BR.
Columbine. British & Continental Music Agencies Ltd.

The remaining works are controlled by Stainer & Bell Ltd.

MONTH'S MIND

. . . days which our ancestors called their 'Month's Mind,' as being the days whereon their souls (after death) were had in special remembrance—hence the expression of 'having a Month's Mind,' to imply a longing desire.

From Brand's "Observations on Popular Antiquities." (London: Chatto & Windus, 1913).

John Ireland

Andante moderato ($\quad$ = 76 - 80)

To Herbert S. Brown

THE CHERRY TREE

"And since to look at things in bloom
Fifty springs are little room,
About the woodlands I will go
To see the cherry hung with snow."
A. E. Housman

JOHN IRELAND

WINTHROP ROGERS EDITION
Copyright 1938 in U.S.A. by Hawkes & Son (London) Ltd.
© Copyright Assigned to H. Freeman & Co. 1959

To Alfred Chenhalls

CYPRESS

"Come away, come away, death,
And in sad cypress let me be laid."

Shakespeare

JOHN IRELAND

WINTHROP ROGERS EDITION
Copyright 1938 in U.S.A. by Hawkes & Son (London) Ltd.
© Copyright Assigned to H. Freeman & Co. 1959

For Harriet Cohen

THE PALM AND MAY

"The Palm and May
make country houses gay."
Thomas Nash

JOHN IRELAND

WINTHROP ROGERS EDITION
Copyright **1938** in U.S.A. by Hawkes & Son (London) Ltd.
© Copyright Assigned to H. Freeman & Co. **1959**

Buoyant *(not faster)*

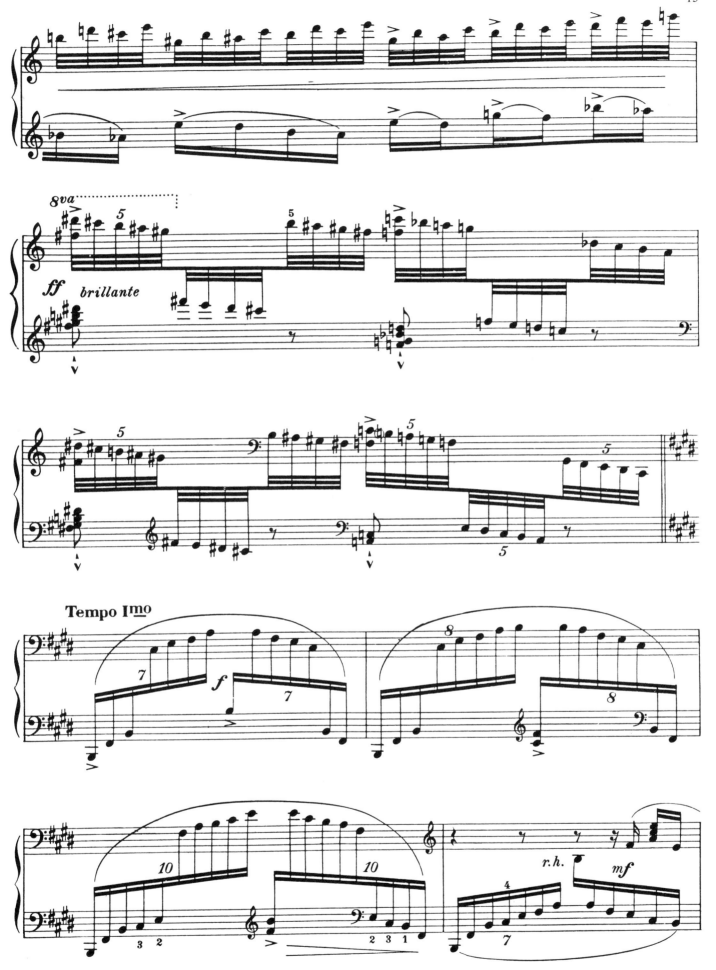

J. I.
Deal, 1937

The Island of Guernsey was known to the Romans, who named it *SARNIA.*—— NATIONAL GAZETTEER

Le Catioroc

Silet per diem universus, nec sine horrore secretus est ; lucet nocturnis ignibus, chorus Ægipanum undique personatur : audiuntur et cantus tibiarum et tinnitus cymbalorum per oram maritimam.

POMPONIUS MELA, " *De Situ Orbis* " *(c. A.D. 50)*

All day long, heavy silence broods, and a certain hidden terror lurks there. But at nightfall gleams the light of fires ; the chorus of Ægipans resounds on every side : the shrilling of flutes and the clash of cymbals re-echo by the waste shores of the sea.

to Alfred Sebire

Le Catioroc

John Ireland

WINTHROP ROGERS EDITION
Copyright **1941** in U.S.A. by Hawkes & Son (London) Ltd.
Copyright for all countries

24

Come prima

Fort Sausmarez, L'Eree, 1940

C'était un de ces jours printaniers où mai se dépense tout entier. Sous toutes les rumeurs, de la forêt comme du village, de la vague comme de l'atmosphère, il y avait un roucoulement.

Les premiers papillons se posaient sur les premières roses. La profonde chanson des arbres était chantée par des oiseaux nés d'hier. Ils chantaient leur premier chant, ils volaient leur premier vol.

Le printemps jetait tout son argent et tout son or dans l'immense panier percé des bois. Les pousses nouvelles étaient toutes fraîches vertes.

Partout une divine plénitude et un gonflement mystérieux faisaient deviner l'effort panique et sacré de la sève en travail.

Qui brillait, brillait plus ; qui aimait, aimait mieux . . . . .

VICTOR HUGO, " *Les Travailleurs de la Mer* "

In a May Morning

JOHN IRELAND

Birnam Court,
St. Peter Port,
May, 1940

Upon the flowery forefront of the year
One wandering by the grey-green April sea
.... Along the foam-flowered strand
Breeze-brightened, ...

SWINBURNE, *"Thalassius"*

To Mrs. Mignot

SONG OF THE SPRINGTIDES

JOHN IRELAND

Un pochettino meno allegro (♩ = 80-84)

J. I. April 1940 – March 1941

A GRECIAN LAD

"A Grecian lad, as I hear tell,
One that many loved in vain,
Looked into a forest well
And never looked away again."

A.E. Housman, 'A Shropshire Lad'

John Ireland

Poco andante (♩ = 54-58 approx.)

PIANO

mp dolce

re-written from an early MS. J.I.

THE BOY BISHOP

'diffusa est gratia in labiis tuis.'
Psalm XLV

John Ireland

PUCK'S BIRTHDAY

'I am that merry wanderer of the night.'
A Midsummer Night's Dream

John Ireland

PIANO

COLUMBINE

20th Century

John Ireland
(England — b.1879)

This piece, as its title implies, has some affinity with the dance and suggests a feminine personality. These two phrases give the clue to its pervading atmosphere. It needs a gentle singing touch and a delicate flexibility which maintains the rhythm without accentuating the "bar-lines."

(a shade slower and more languorous)

Printed in Great Britain by Galliard (Printers) Ltd Great Yarmouth